About Skill Builders Reading

by R.B. Snow and Ruby Klenk

Welcome to RBP Books' Skill Builders series. Like our Summer Bridge Activities collection, the Skill Builders series is designed to make learning both fun and rewarding.

This workbook holds students' interest with the right mix of humor, imagination, and instruction as they steadily improve their reading comprehension and other skills. The diverse assignments enhance reading skills while giving students something fun to think about—from Betsy Ross to birds. As students complete the workbook, they will enhance their reading comprehension.

A critical thinking section includes exercises to help develop higher-order thinking skills.

Learning is more effective when approached with an element of fun and enthusiasm—just as most children approach life. That's why the Skill Builders combine entertaining and academically sound exercises with eye-catching graphics and fun themes—to make reviewing basic skills at school or home fun and effective, for both you and your budding scholars.

Table of Contents

Teach Me 4–5
Agent Apple 6–7
An Ordinary Day 8–9
Bubble Fun 10–11
Changing with the Seasons 12–13
The Library 14–15
The Wind 16–17
Bicycle Safety 18–19
Heroes 20–21
A Prize Pie 22–23
Telling Time 24–25
Grandpa Remembers 26–27
Heroes of Long Ago 28–29
Ben Franklin 30–31
Betsy Ross. 32–33
Martin Luther King, Jr. 34–35
Animal Poem 36–37
The Birds in My Garden .38–39
Neighborhood Heroes 40–41
Animals' Sleeping Habits 42–43
Briauna's Favorite Place. .44–45
Birds. 46–47
The Roller Coaster 48–49
Fairy Tales 50–51
Sweet Porridge. 52–53
Riddle Me This 54–55
The Ladybug 56–57
Florida 58–59
Ellis Island. 60–61
Chinese Immigrants 62–63
Ling-Shau Yu's Journal 64–65
Critical Thinking Skills. 66–74
Answer Pages 75–78

3rd Grade Suggested Reading List

Adler, David
Cam Jansen and
the Mystery of the
Television Dog

Barrett, Judi
Cloudy With a Chance
of Meatballs

Berenstain, Stan and Jan
Berenstain Bears
chapter books
Accept No Substitutes

Burton, Virginia Lee
Katy and the Big Snow

Catling, Patrick Skene
Chocolate Touch

Cleary, Beverly
Ramona Quimby:
Age 8

Cole, Joanna
Magic School Bus
series

Danziger, Paula
There's a Bat in Bunk
Five

Donnelly, Judy
Veterans Memorial
Moonwalk: First Trip to
the Moon

Ernst, Lisa Campbell
Nattie Parson's Good
Luck Lamb

Fox, Paula
Maurice's Room

Gleiter, Jan
Paul Revere

Graff, Stewart
Helen Keller:
Toward the Light

Gutelle, Andrew
Baseball's Best:
Five True Stories

Havill, Juanita
Treasure Nap

Hidaka, Masako
Girl from the Snow
Country

Jeschke, Susan
Perfect the Pig

Jonas, Ann
Aardvarks, Disembark!

Jukes, Mavis
Blackberries in the
Dark

Kellogg, Steven
Paul Bunyan
Best Friends

Konigsburg, E. L.
The View from
Saturday

Krensky, Stephen
Witch Hunt

Little, Emily
Trojan Horse

Lobel, Arnold
Grasshopper on
the Road
Book of Pigericks

McMullan, Kate
Dinosaur Hunters

Osborne, Mary Pope
Moonhorse

Raskin, Ellen
Nothing Ever Happens
on My Block

Schroeder, Alan
A Story of Young
Harriet Tubman

**Sharmat, Marjorie
Weinman**
Nate the Great series

Smith, Robert Kimmer
Chocolate Fever

Sobol, Donald J.
Encyclopedia Brown
series

Stadler, John
Animal Cafe

Steig, William
The Amazing Bone
Amos and Boris
Sylvester and the
Magic Pebble

Stock, Catherine
Emma's Dragon Hunt

Stoutenburg, Adrien
American Tall Tales

Waber, Bernard
Lyle, Lyle, Crocodile

White, E.B.
Charlotte's Web

Teach Me

Don't tell me that I can't, or I won't.
Always tell me to try, and I will.

Teach me to smile when I am sad.
Teach me to talk when I am mad.

Teach me to soar and teach me to fly.
Answer my questions when I ask why.

Teach me that failures are successes not tried.
Teach me to open my arms up wide.

Teach me to love and to laugh and to live.
Teach me to work and to share and to give.

Teach me so that I become all I can be.
Then stand back and be proud of me.

Reading Comprehension

1. Who is this poem written by and to?

   A. by a child, to a parent or teacher

   B. by a child, to a friend

   C. by a teacher, to a student

2. Put an X next to those things below that should not be taught.

   _____ how to hit someone

   _____ how to sing

   _____ how to grow flowers

   _____ how to call someone names

   _____ how to scream and shout when you are upset

3. Draw a line between the opposites.

laugh	get
love	happy
work	cry
give	rest
sad	hate

4. What is the opposite of <u>failure</u>?

   _____

© RBP Books

Agent Apple: Your mission, should you choose to accept it, will require you to give your all.

First, you must infiltrate the mouth to be crushed by the teeth and broken down by saliva. Then, you will move down the esophagus toward the target area: the small intestine. But first you must battle through the stomach. There you will have to face the dreaded stomach acid! If you are successful, you will have about four hours to begin deconstruction.

Now comes the vital part of your mission as you enter the small intestines. During your twenty-foot ride you must release calcium for bones, vitamin C and folic acid for the immune system and cell growth, as well as potassium for muscles, and fiber for digestion.

Remember, Agent Apple, the health of your target demands that you give this mission all you've got!

6

1. What is this story about?

    A. It is a description of digestion.

    B. Agents must give all they've got.

    C. Apples are good for you.

2. Write down the five things the apple will give to the body once it is digested.

    _____

    _____

    _____

3. Where does Agent Apple go first?

    A. into the mouth

    B. through the stomach

    C. into the small intestines

4. What does infiltrate mean?

    A. enter

    B. absorb

    C. slide

5. Write another title for this story.

_____

An Ordinary Day

Rachel was walking out of the school building looking sad. Her mother was waiting for her. "Hey, why the long face?" her mother asked.

"Today was boring," replied Rachel. "There were no tests, nothing special for lunch, no extra recesses, no special programs. It was just an <u>ordinary</u> day."

"But it's the ordinary days that make the exciting days seem exciting. If we didn't have ordinary days, we would never notice the exciting days," Rachel's mother explained.

Rachel thought about what her mother said. Maybe ordinary days were as special as exciting days.

1. What does <u>ordinary</u> mean?

    A. plain, the same as everything else

    B. unique and different

    C. strong

    D. special

2. What did Rachel learn?

    A. Her mother had a bad day, too.

    B. Everyone has a bad day sometimes.

    C. Ordinary days make exciting days more exciting.

3. What does the phrase "long face" mean?

    A. a happy look

    B. an excited look

    C. a sad look

4. What would make your day at school exciting?

_____

_____

_____

_____

_____

_____

_____

Bubble Fun

Kate and Nicole decided to wash the car. They gathered sponges, rags, and a bucket of soapy water. Kate put her sponge into the soapy water. She noticed bubbles coming from the bucket. They were large and clear. "Look at the bubbles!" Kate exclaimed. The bubbles gave Nicole an idea. She ran inside.

She came back with a bottle of corn syrup, a <u>slotted</u> <u>spoon</u>, and several wire coat hangers. Kate watched closely as Nicole poured the syrup into the soapy water. Then Nicole dipped the slotted spoon into the bucket. She waved the spoon around. Bubbles floated everywhere. Kate caught a bubble. She held it in her hand. It didn't pop! The corn syrup made the bubbles stronger. Then Nicole showed Kate how to bend a wire hanger into a bubble wand.

The girls had so much fun, they forgot about washing the car. Nicole's dad saw the fun the girls were having. He finished washing the car. Then he joined the girls for some bubble fun.

10

Reading Comprehension

1. What is the main idea of this story?
   A. This is how to wash a car.
   B. If you wait long enough, someone else will do your chores.
   C. Making bubbles is fun.
   D. Summer is fun.

2. Number the sentences in the order they happened in the story.

   _____ Nicole poured corn syrup in the soapy water.

   _____ Dad joined the girls for some bubble fun.

   _____ Kate noticed the bubbles coming from the bucket.

   _____ The girls had fun making bubbles.

   _____ Nicole ran inside to get corn syrup, a slotted spoon, and wire coat hangers.

3. What is a slotted spoon?
   A. a spoon used only to blow bubbles
   B. a very large spoon
   C. a wooden spoon
   D. a spoon with holes in it

4. Who finished washing the car?

   _____

5. Write T if the sentence is true and F if the sentence is false.

   _____ Kate dipped the spoon into the bucket.

   _____ Nicole finished washing the car.

   _____ Dad joined the girls for some bubble fun.

   _____ The coat hangers made the bubbles stronger.

Changing with the Seasons

We are not the only ones to change our clothes with the seasons. Some animals change how they look, too. They seem to know the temperature will make a difference.

The arctic fox has a white fur coat in the winter. It is not easy to see him in the snow. When spring comes, his white fur changes to brown. It is now the color of the ground.

One type of bird has white feathers in the winter. It, too, is hard to see in the snow. In the springtime, the bird <u>molts</u>. This means it sheds all of its feathers. The bird grows new feathers that are speckled. When the bird is very still, it looks like a rock.

We change our dress with the seasons to protect us from the weather. Animals do the same to protect themselves from their enemies.

12

Reading Comprehension

1. What is this story mostly about?
    A. how people change
    B. how animals change
    C. where animals live
    D. how animals scare their enemies

2. What color is the arctic fox's fur in the winter?
    A. purple
    B. brown
    C. red
    D. white

3. What happens to the bird in the story in the spring?
    A. Its feathers fall out.
    B. It flies north.
    C. Its feathers turn red.
    D. It looks for its old nest.

4. The word <u>molts</u> means
    A. change.
    B. to give up.
    C. to shed feathers.
    D. to hide from an enemy.

5. You can probably guess that
    A. animals like their enemies.
    B. it is not always easy to see an animal.
    C. it is easy to catch most animals.
    D. animals never change.

The Library

Jen was new in town. Her family had just moved from the country. Jen's new house was just down the street from the public library. Jen had never been to a public library before. She had only been to the  small library at her old school. But this library was a large, three-story building. From the outside, Jen thought it looked a bit scary.

However, Jen loved books so much that she got up enough courage to go inside. As she walked in the door, Jen stopped. She looked all around. She had never seen so many books at one time. Jen felt a little <u>overwhelmed</u>. Marie, one of the librarians, noticed Jen standing frozen by the front door. She offered to show Jen around the library. Marie took Jen up the elevator to the third floor, where the children's library was. Marie showed Jen how the books were shelved and how to <u>locate</u> her favorite authors. Then Marie showed Jen the computers that were used to locate books. At Jen's old school library, she used a card catalog to find books. The computer made it much simpler. Jen spent hours looking through the books. Finally, Jen chose a mystery book to check out.

Jen took the book with her to the first floor. She walked to the checkout counter. Marie greeted her with a smile. She

helped Jen fill out an application for a library card. Then she helped Jen check her book out. As Jen walked out of the library with her book in hand, she knew she had found a new favorite place.

14

1. Where were the children's books found?
  A. on the first floor
  B. on the second floor
  C. on the third floor

2. Why did Jen think the library looked a bit scary?
  A. The library was dirty and run down.
  B. The library was far away from her house.
  C. The library was a large, three-story building.

3. What does <u>overwhelmed</u> mean in this story?
  A. not sure where to go or what to do first
  B. scared
  C. happy to be there

4. Write a synonym for <u>locate</u>.

_____

5. How did Jen feel as she left the library?

_____

15

The Wind by Robert Louis Stevenson

I saw you toss the kites on high

And blow the birds about the sky;

And all around I heard you pass,

Like ladies' skirts across the grass—

    O wind, a-blowing all day long,

    O wind, that sings so loud a song!

I saw the different things you did,

But always you yourself you hid.

I felt you push, I heard you call,

I could not see yourself at all—

    O wind, a-blowing all day long,

    O wind, that sings so loud a song!

O you that are so strong and cold,

O blower, are you young or old?

Are you a beast of field and tree,

Or just a stronger child than me?

    O wind, a-blowing all day long,

    O wind, that sings so loud a song!

1. What is this poem about?
   A. blowing birds around the sky
   B. the wind
   C. doing different things
   D. blowing hot or cold

2. What line is repeated more than once in the poem?
   A. *O wind, a-blowing all day long*
   B. *And all around I heard you pass*
   C. *I felt you push, I heard you call*
   D. *O you that are so strong and cold*

3. What does the author want to know about the wind?
   A. What causes wind?
   B. How strong is the wind?
   C. How does the wind sing so loud?
   D. Is the wind young or old?

4. What is the wind compared to?
   A. kites in the sky
   B. ladies' skirts across the grass
   C. a child
   D. birds in the sky

Riding a bicycle can be fun. You get a sense of pride from learning to ride without training wheels. You also get a sense of freedom from riding your bike to explore new places. Unfortunately, every year children get hurt in bike accidents. It is important to learn and follow some bicycle safety rules.

First, make sure your bicycle is working properly. Check the brakes. Be sure that they stop the bike easily. The handlebars and the pedals should be tightly secure. If any part is not in good working order, fix it before riding the bike.

Next, check your safety equipment. Be sure that your bike has reflectors. Reflectors help drivers and other riders see you. Be sure to wear a bicycle helmet. Bicycle helmets will protect your head if you fall off the bicycle. You should always wear shoes when riding a bike. Check that your shoelaces are tied so that they don't get tangled up with the pedals.

Once you have checked your bicycle and your safety equipment, you are ready to ride. Always ride your bike in the direction of traffic. Use bike paths whenever possible. Otherwise, stay close to the side of the road. Follow all traffic signs. Use arm signals to tell others you are making a turn. Pay attention. Be aware. Car drivers don't always pay attention to bicycle riders, so make sure you are aware of the dangers around you.

1. What is the main idea of this story?

A. Wearing your helmet is important.

B. Cars don't watch for bicycle riders.

C. Follow the bicycle safety rules.

2. Circle the compound words found in this story.

3. Use the correct homonym in each sentence.

Check the_____on your bike.

(brakes, breaks)

Use common_____when riding your bike.

(cents, sense)

Be sure the_____on your bike are tight.

(pedals, petals)

Ride on the right side of the_____.

(rode, road)

4. Why is it important to follow bicycle safety rules?

_____

_____

_____

Heroes

Heroes are people like you and me,
who choose to act selflessly.

Heroes give all they have, then give some more.
Heroes take action when action's called for.

Heroes pick themselves up when they make mistakes.
Heroes keep trying. They've got what it takes.

Heroes are willing to give their all,
They stop, look, and listen, then answer the call.

We look to heroes to show us the way
To go the extra mile, to seize the day.

So be kind and helpful
    wherever you go,
For someone may look to
    you as a hero.

1. What is the main idea of this story?

  A. Not everybody can be a hero.

  B. Anyone can be a hero if he or she tries.

  C. Heroes take action when needed.

2. Explain what a hero is.

  _____

  _____

3. What is the opposite of <u>selflessly</u>?

  A. selfishly

  B. happily

  C. selfless

  D. shyly

4. "Give it their all," "go the extra mile," and "seize the day" are all sayings that mean what?

  A. Be a good friend.

  B. Never give up.

  C. Believe in yourself.

5. Who is your hero? Draw a picture of him or her.

  _____

A Prize Pie

Sue and her mother always baked cherry pies for the county fair. The fair was in exactly one month, and the plans for the "best cherry pie ever" were already in motion. Sue and her mother tried making their famous pie with fresh cherries from their cherry trees. They also tried using canned cherries. Sue liked the pie with the fresh cherries best.

They also tried making different types of crust. The first type of crust they made was thick and doughy. The second crust was more flaky. The top of the pie was made of strips of pie dough woven over and under each other to create a lattice look. After both pies were finished, Sue and her mother asked the family's opinion. They decided the one with flaky, lattice crust and fresh cherry filling was the best pie.

Sue and her mother practiced one more time, and the pie turned out terrific. They were ready for the pie contest. Sue and her mother won second place!

22

1. What type of crust did Sue and her mother decide to use for the fair?

   A. They used a thick and doughy one.

   B. They used a flaky, lattice-looking one.

   C. They used a puffy one.

   D. They didn't use a crust on top at all.

2. Which pie did their family like the most?

   A. the thick and doughy crust with the canned cherries

   B. the flaky, lattice crust with fresh cherries

   C. the flaky, lattice crust with frozen cherries

   D. the thick and doughy crust with fresh cherries

3. Make the following words plural.

   pie   _____

   cherry   _____

   family   _____

   contest _____

   wash   _____

   dish   _____

4. Do you think their pie was good? Draw your favorite kind of pie.

   _____

Cavemen first told time by watching the sun rise and set. They got up with the sun and went to bed with the sun. They never worried about the time of day. They ate when they were hungry. They survived by doing what they needed to do. They never needed a clock.

Time became more important as people became more civilized. They watched the sun more closely. It was noon when the sun was in the middle of the sky. It was time to quit work when the sun was setting in the west.

The sun's shadow became important for telling the time of day. Only a straight stick was needed. It was placed straight up in an open space. The stick made a shadow. The shadow made a path all around the stick. The path was divided into 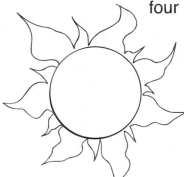 four equal parts. The end of the shadow told the time of day. The stick's shadow was shortest at noon. This method of telling time led to the invention of the sundial.

1. What was the only thing needed to tell time by the sun's shadow?

_____

2. How was the stick placed in the ground?

_____

3. What was the length of the shadow at noon?

    A. longest

    B. shortest

    C. next to longest

    D. none of the above

4. What instrument was invented to tell time from the sun's shadow?

    A. sundial

    B. digital clock

    C. watch

    D. clock

5. Place a straight stick in a clearing outside and see if you can tell what time it is. Write what happens.

_____

_____

_____

_____

Grandpa Remembers

My grandpa lives just down the lane and around the corner from my family. I love to go to his house. Time always flies with my grandpa. Grandpa loves to tell stories about how things used to be. He always says he hopes he doesn't talk my ear off, but I love to listen to his stories. Here's one of them.

"One nippy winter day, when I wasn't much older than you," Grandpa began, "I begged to go with my dad to harvest a crop of ice blocks. When I was young, my family didn't have refrigerators like we do now. Gathering ice blocks was the only way to keep foods cold through the spring and summer.

"I helped my dad get the tractor and wagon hooked up. Then down to the river we went. When we got there, Dad took out the logging saw. A logging saw is a long saw with handles at each end. Usually a logging saw is used to cut trees, but in the winter it's good for cutting ice blocks. I watched my dad put the saw in the water. Pushing and pulling, he cut a long slab of ice. We worked together to cut the slab into square blocks. Then my dad used ice tongs to put the blocks of ice on the wagon. When they were loaded, we hit the road and headed to the ice shed. The ice shed had three or four inches of sawdust on the floor. We put the blocks on top of the saw-dust. Then we packed more sawdust around the blocks. We stored all of our ice cream and other foods that needed to stay cold inside the ice shed."

It is fun to shoot the breeze with Grandpa and learn about how things were when he was my age. I will always remember our "remembering" times. Someday it will be fun to have "remembering" times of my own.

26

Reading Comprehension

1. What is a <u>knight</u>?

_____

2. What is a <u>maiden</u>?

_____

3. What is a <u>joust</u>?
   A. a contest at a tournament where two knights would battle with long spears
   B. the knight's suit of armor, which was a symbol of honor, valor, and chivalry
   C. the prize for winning the battle

4. What is a <u>code</u> <u>of</u> <u>conduct</u>?
   A. a secret language knights used
   B. a set of rules knights had to follow
   C. a contest in a tournament

5. Circle the silent letter in each word.

   k n i g h t

   k n o w

   k n o c k

   c o d e

   r u l e

   c o m p e t e

Ben Franklin

Benjamin Franklin was born January 17, 1705. He was a printer, a statesman, and an inventor.

At the age of 17, Ben Franklin began working as a printer. He printed newspapers and books. He wrote many of the things he printed. In 1732, Franklin wrote and published <u>Poor Richard's Almanac</u>. He also printed all the money for the state of Pennsylvania.

Ben Franklin worked hard to make Pennsylvania a better place. He made improvements in the postal system and the police force. He established the first public library. He also helped start the first fire station after a fire destroyed much of the city of Philadelphia. He was elected delegate of Pennsylvania to the second Continental Congress in 1775. In 1776, he helped write the Declaration of Independence.

Franklin was also an inventor. He was always thinking of ways to do things faster and better. In 1741, he invented a stove that would heat and stay at a certain temperature. He invented a type of glasses that he could use to help him read in his old age. He is probably best known for the important discoveries he made with electricity in 1752.

Benjamin Franklin died April 17, 1790, at the age of 84. More than 20,000 people attended his funeral. He was an American hero who is still remembered today.

1. Put an X by the things that are true about Benjamin Franklin.

   _____ He wrote books and newspaper articles.

   _____ He worked as a mail carrier.

   _____ He was the president of the United States.

   _____ He helped write the Declaration of Independence.

   _____ He made important discoveries about electricity.

2. What was Benjamin Franklin's contribution in 1776?

   _____

3. Number the events in the order they occurred in Benjamin Franklin's life.

   _____ He died at the age of 84.

   _____ He became delegate of Pennsylvania.

   _____ He worked as a printer.

   _____ He was born on January 17, 1705.

   _____ He made important discoveries about electricity.

4. Write down why you think Benjamin Franklin was a hero.

   _____

   _____

   _____

   _____

Betsy Ross

Betsy Ross is known as an American hero. She did not fight in wars. She did not become president. She was simply a seamstress. But her contribution to our country is still remembered today. Betsy Ross made the first United States flag.

In her journal, Betsy Ross wrote about a meeting with George Washington in May of 1776. Betsy attended the same church as George Washington. George Washington, who was a general at the time, asked Betsy to create a new flag for the new country that would soon earn its independence. In July of 1776, the Declaration of Independence declared that the United States was independent from Britain. On June 14, 1777, it was decided that the flag Betsy Ross made would be the flag of the United States. The flag was to represent the unity of the 13 colonies as one country. The new flag was first flown over Fort Stanwix, New York, on August 3, 1777.

Today, our flag has 50 stars representing the 50 states. The 13 stripes represent the 13 original colonies. Our flag represents the freedoms we enjoy. We continue to honor the flag and the freedom it represents by saying the Pledge of Allegiance and singing "The Star-Spangled Banner." We even have set aside June 14th as Flag Day to honor the flag.

1. What is Betsy Ross best remembered for?
   A. fighting in a war
   B. marrying the president
   C. making the first American flag

2. Underline the sentence below that is true.
   A. The stars on the flag represent the 50 states, and the stripes represent the 13 colonies.
   B. The stars on the flag represent the 50 states, and the stripes represent the number of battles won to gain our independence.
   C. The stars on the flag represent the 50 heroes of the war, and the stripes represent the 13 colonies.

3. Why is Betsy Ross an American hero?
   A. She made the American flag.
   B. She married the president.
   C. She was the first woman in Congress.

4. What kind of flag would you have if you had your own country? Draw it here.

Bonus! Do you know how many stars the first American flag had?_____

How many stars does it have now?_____

Martin Luther King, Jr.

Martin Luther King, Jr. was a hero. He worked hard for racial equality. He was born on January 15, 1929.

"Free at last! Free at last!"

Young Martin was a good student. His mother taught him to read before he started school. He skipped several grades and entered college at age 15. After graduating from college, he married Corretta Scott. He became a minister.

In the 1950s, Martin joined the civil rights movement. This movement called for equality for African Americans. He led many peaceful <u>demonstrations</u> and spoke out against racism. In 1963, King gave his famous "I Have a Dream" speech.

In 1964, Congress passed the Civil Rights Act, making segregation against the law. In 1964, Martin Luther King, Jr. was awarded the Nobel Peace Prize.

On April 4, 1968, while visiting Memphis, Tennessee, Martin Luther King, Jr. was shot to death. We celebrate the life of this American hero each year on the third Monday of January.

1. What is Martin Luther King, Jr. best remembered for?
   A. being a good student
   B. working hard for racial equality
   C. winning the Nobel Peace Prize

2. Write the base word.

   graduation   _____

   celebration   _____

   demonstration   _____

   segregation   _____

3. What is Martin Luther King's famous speech called?

   _____

4. What are <u>demonstrations</u>?
   A. people gathering to protest
   B. people rioting in the streets
   C. people going to each other's houses

5. What do you think would make the world a better place for all people?

   _____

   _____

   _____

   _____

   _____

Animal Poem

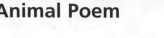

How many animals can you name?
This seems like a never-ending game.

There are little ants so very small.
There are spotted giraffes so very tall.

There are mammals and
insects, to name a few.
There are reptiles and
<u>amphibians</u> in the zoo.

There are animals that fly and some that can walk.
There are cows in a herd and birds in a flock.

There are animals that live on land
and some that live in the seas.
There are animals that live in the
ground and some that live in trees.

There are animals that are wild and some that are tame.
There are just too many animals for us to even name.

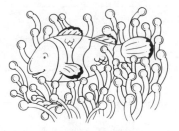

36

1. What is the main idea of this poem?

    A. There are too many animals to name.

    B. Animals make great pets.

    C. Some animals are wild, and some are tame.

2. Draw a line between the opposites.

    land   tame

    ground   sky

    wild   tall

    few   sea

    small   many

3. Write down all the rhyming words found in this poem.

_____ _____ _____

_____ _____ _____

_____ _____ _____

_____ _____ _____

4. What is an <u>amphibian</u>?

    A. a cold-blooded animal that lives on land and in water

    B. an animal that is warm blooded

    C. an animal that has feathers and can fly

5. See how many different animal names you can write down in one minute.

_____

_____

_____

The Birds in My Garden

I like to watch the birds in my garden. The robins come as the snow is melting. The male robin has a red breast. He helped his mate build a nest in the cherry tree. I peeked into the nest. I counted three tiny eggs.

Two magpies live in my garden. Their feathers are shiny black and white. The magpies built their huge nest in the pine tree. Magpies can copy the sounds of other birds. They are noisy and sometimes quarrel.

My favorite birds to watch are quail. They have a topknot on their head that bobs when they walk. Quail make their nests on the ground under a bush. They live in families called flocks. They can run very fast. When they are frightened, they scatter to different places. When the danger is gone, they whistle to each other to come back. I love watching the baby quail follow their parents. Sometimes, I see them in the road, and I worry they might get hit by a car. They seem to always scatter just in time.

1. What does the child in this story like to do?
   A. watch birds
   B. play with the dog
   C. play with the cat
   D. pet birds

2. Which bird is <u>not</u> in the garden?
   A. magpie
   B. lark
   C. robin
   D. quail

3. Where do quails make their nests?
   A. in a cherry tree
   B. in a birdhouse
   C. in a pine tree
   D. on the ground under a bush

4. What does the word <u>flock</u> mean?
   A. a group of birds
   B. a group of cows
   C. a group of dogs
   D. a group of kittens

Neighborhood Heroes

Life was pretty dull around our quiet neighborhood. So a couple of friends and I decided to become neighborhood news reporters. Maybe if we looked for news, we'd find it. We used my tree house for our headquarters. We set up our headquarters with pencils, notebooks, clipboards, binoculars, and even a laptop computer and a cell phone. We began discussing topics we might want to report on. Max was looking through the binoculars. "Looks like we might have our first story," he said. "Georgie Willows is sitting on his front steps crying. You guys keep talking. I'll go see what's wrong with Georgie."

Soon Max was back. He wanted us to help him. "Georgie's hamster got loose in his yard. He can't find it anywhere." We all went to help. We looked everywhere. Suddenly we heard the dog next door barking. When we went to investigate, sure enough, the neighbor's dog had Georgie's hamster cornered in the garage. We rescued the frightened hamster and took him back to Georgie.

We went back to the tree house. This time I was looking over the neighborhood with the binoculars. As I looked over into Mrs. Stevens's backyard, I saw her lying by her garden, clutching her chest. "Someone call 911. I think Mrs. Stevens is in trouble!" I yelled. Max called 911 while the rest of us ran to Mrs. Stevens. Mrs. Stevens wasn't moving. Last summer I had taken a first aid class and learned CPR. I started CPR on Mrs. Stevens. Soon the ambulance arrived! The paramedics were able to revive Mrs. Stevens. They took her to the hospital. Mrs. Stevens had had a heart attack, but our quick thinking saved her life. The local newspaper wrote an article about what happened. The article called us heroes. So now instead of being the neighborhood reporters, we are known as the neighborhood heroes.

1. Why did the friends become neighborhood news reporters?

   A. They were bored.

   B. They wanted to get some writing experience.

   C. They liked news.

2. Circle all the compound words in this story.

3. A <u>synonym</u> is a word that means the same as another word. An <u>antonym</u> is a word that means the opposite of another word. Write whether each pair of words are synonyms or antonyms.

dull	boring	_____
quiet	loud	_____
rescued	saved	_____
frightened	courageous	_____
exciting	dull	_____
scared	frightened	_____

4. Why are the friends the neighborhood heroes?

   _____

   _____

   _____

Briauna's Favorite Place

Briauna lives in Newfoundland, Canada. She is at her favorite place. It is a high cliff that overlooks the ocean. She likes to watch the fishing boats bob like corks on the blue water. She listens to the cries of the seagulls as they look for food. She admires the beauty of the tall lighthouse. She laughs as she watches the whales play. Briauna lies on her back. She finds animals in the clouds. It is a peaceful day.

Suddenly, a huge wave crashes onto the shore. Briauna sits up and looks at the ocean. She watches as the fishing boats start coming to port as fast as they can. The clouds darken. A strong wind begins to blow. A foghorn cries out. It warns the seamen a storm is coming. The waves get bigger and bigger.

At first, sailors thought giant sea monsters made the waves rise high over their boats. Now they know it is the weather that causes the huge waves.

As the storm comes in, Briauna is glad she is on her cliff high above the angry ocean. She takes one last look at the beautiful, white-capped waves. Then she quickly runs home.

1. What is the main idea of this story?
   A. sailors and whales
   B. The weather can change quickly.
   C. Sailors are not afraid of the storms.
   D. a favorite place

2. What did the fishing boats look like on the ocean?
   A. speedboats
   B. bobbing corks
   C. sinking ships
   D. big ships

3. What did the sailors believe caused the giant waves?
   A. giant sea monsters
   B. bad luck
   C. whales playing
   D. none of the above

4. Find and write another word for sea.

   _____

5. You can guess that _____.
   A. sailing in a storm is fun
   B. animals cause storms
   C. Briauna loves the sea
   D. fishing is best during a storm

Animals' Sleeping Habits

Sleep for humans almost always means a bed or a mat. Animals, however, have many different ways of sleeping.

For warmth, some animals sleep in groups. Lions, monkeys, and penguins are a few animals that sleep in groups. Elephants also sleep in a group, but they sleep in groups for protection. The larger elephants make a circle around the young elephants. The larger elephants sleep standing up. The younger ones get inside the circle and lie down to sleep.

Some animals sleep in trees. Birds will lock their feet onto a branch to keep from falling out of the tree. Other animals, like squirrels and baboons, make nests in the trees to sleep in. They curl up to keep warm. Bats hang upside down from tree branches to sleep.

Most animals look for warm, dry places to sleep. But ducks often sleep in the water. Sea otters sleep in the water, too. They float on their backs in the seaweed.

Most animals lie down to sleep. However, some large animals, like horses, sleep standing up. The flamingo sleeps standing on just one leg.

Most animals sleep at night, but some animals are nocturnal. Nocturnal animals sleep during the day. Bats are nocturnal animals. They wake up when the sun goes down.

Animals sleep in many different places and in many different ways. But just like humans, every animal must sleep.

1. Which sentence tells the main idea of this story?
   A. Sleep for humans almost always means a bed or a mat.
   B. Animals have many different ways of sleeping.
   C. Most animals sleep at night.

2. Put a **T** by the sentences that are true and an **F** by the sentences that are false.

   _____ All animals sleep at night.

   _____ Elephants sleep in groups for protection.

   _____ Birds are the only animals that build nests.

   _____ All animals sleep.

3. Draw a line between the animals and the way they sleep.

   elephants   standing on one foot

   otters   in nests in trees

   bats   upside down

   flamingos   floating on their backs

   squirrels   in groups

4. How and where do you sleep?

   _____

   _____

Birds are unique animals. Birds have wings, feathers, and a beak. Birds are the only animals that have feathers. These feathers <u>enable</u> most birds to fly. Their ability to fly helps them stay alive. Their ability to fly helps them hunt for food, escape their enemies, and <u>migrate</u> away from bad weather. Feathers also protect the bird from getting too hot or too cold. Birds have beaks, but they do not have teeth. They use their beaks to get food. Birds eat insects, worms, seeds, and grains.

Birds are protective parents. Birds lay eggs. They build nests to protect their eggs. Usually the mother bird sits on the nest, keeping the eggs warm. Sometimes the mother and father bird take turns. Both the mother and father bird keep watch on the nest before the eggs hatch. The nests keep the baby birds warm after they hatch from their eggs. The adult birds take care of the baby birds until they are ready to fly. The parents bring food to the baby birds in the nest.

1. Which sentence tells the main idea of this story?
   A. Birds are unique animals.
   B. The adult bird teaches its babies how to fly, find food, and build nests.
   C. Birds are one of the few animals that lay eggs.

2. Finish the sentences below.

   Birds are the only animals that have_____.

   Birds have _____ but do not have_____.

   Birds are_____parents.

3. What does the word <u>enable</u> mean?
   A. to make possible
   B. to make it impossible
   C. to change

4. What does the word <u>migrate</u> mean?
   A. to hide under trees
   B. to fly to other places
   C. to find shelter

5. Draw a picture of your favorite bird.

The Roller Coaster

The roller coaster's like a snake,
coiling 'round and 'round.
As the cars make their way up,
my heart begins to pound.

The drop comes so quickly
I can't scream or yell.
The whipping of the curves
swings me like a bell.

As the ride comes to an end,
I start to smile and laugh.
I shout, "Let's go again
along that whipping path."

1. Why can't the riders scream or yell?

  A. They will get into trouble.

  B. The roller coaster is going too fast.

  C. They lost their voices.

2. What is the roller coaster compared to in this story?

  A. a river

  B. a snake

  C. a piece of string

  D. a rubber band

3. Did the riders like going on the roller coaster?

  _____

4. Why do you think they call it a roller coaster?

  _____

  _____

  _____

  _____

Fairy Tales

Come, read with me a fairy tale;
Board my ship and let's set sail.

Let's go to once upon a time,
Where good is good and all words rhyme.

Come, follow me to places afar,
beyond the moon, beyond the stars.

We'll travel to lands far away,
Where elves and fairies hide and play.

We'll pretend to be pirates at sea,
Seeking adventure, wild and free.

To where things aren't as they seem,
To places we can only dream.

Reading Comprehension

1. What is a fairy tale?
   A. a make-believe story
   B. a lie
   C. a story about fairies
   D. a story written by fairies

2. Some words have more than one meaning. Read each sentence. Write the letter of the correct definition of each underlined word.

   ___ We used <u>boards</u> to build the ship.

   ___ The man <u>boards</u> the ship with his bags.

       A. to get on a ship   B. pieces of wood

   ___ The <u>star</u> twinkled in the sky.

   ___ He is the <u>star</u> of the show.

       C. a light in the sky   D. the lead actor

   ___ They set <u>sail</u> for a long trip over the ocean.

   ___ They made a <u>sail</u> for their boat.

       E. a piece of material used to propel a boat

       F. to float on the water

3. Write the singular for each word listed below.
   elves_____   pirates_____
   fairies_____   places_____

4. Make up your own fairy tale!

   _____

   _____

   _____

   _____

51

Sweet Porridge

There was a poor but good little girl who lived with her mother in a small little house. One morning the mother went to the cupboard to find something to eat. But the cupboard was bare. The mother sent the little girl into the forest to find some wild blueberries to eat.

While looking for berries, the girl met a woman. The woman was old and bent. She wore rags. She looked as if she hadn't eaten in days. The little girl felt sorry for the old woman. She gave the old woman all of her berries. As the woman ate the berries, something began to happen. The bent, old woman changed into a beautiful <u>enchanted</u> fairy. The little girl could not believe her eyes.

"You have shown great kindness," said the enchanted fairy. "For your kindness, I will give you this magic pot. When the magic words are said, sweet porridge will appear in the pot. With this magic pot you will never be hungry again. Simply say,

"Cook, little pot, cook.
Give us something to eat.
Cook, little pot, cook.
Give us something sweet."

The little girl thanked the fairy and took the pot home to her mother. The mother and the little girl were never hungry again. Instead, they ate sweet porridge whenever they chose.

1. Is this story real or make-believe?

   _____

2. What does <u>enchanted</u> mean?
   A. magical
   B. chanting or singing
   C. mean

3. What does the idiom "the cupboard was bare" mean?
   A. The cupboard was hungry.
   B. The cupboard was naked.
   C. There was no food in the house.
   D. There was a lot of food in the house but none in the cupboards.

4. Why do you think the fairy gave the girl the magic pot?

   _____

   _____

5. If you had a magical pot that could only make one food, what would that food be? Why?

   _____

   _____

   _____

   _____

   _____

Riddle Me This

Riddle me this, riddle me that.
Why is a cat not a bat or a rat?
Or a flea not a bee, a shark not a <u>lark</u>?
And why do we say no light means it's dark?
What makes a train not a car or a plane?
And why call it a train come sunshine or rain?
Why not call it a creeper or super-fast,
    super-sleek, big, squeaky chugger?
It's a train for your sister, your mom, and your dad,
A train for Aunt Sue, Uncle Joe, Cousin Brad.
It's a train in Egypt, France, and St. Paul,
No matter its course or what it might <u>haul</u>.
When it leaves the station or rounds the bend,
A train is a train and to this riddle, no end.
We're told it's a train, so a train it shall be.
But I'll tell you a secret, just between you and me,
I prefer super-fast, super-sleek, big, squeaky chugger!

1. What was another name for the train in this story?

_____

_____

2. What does the word <u>haul</u> mean?

    A. throw

    B. chug

    C. carry

3. What is a lark?

    A. a bird

    B. a snake

    C. a boat

4. What are trains used for?

_____

_____

_____

_____

_____

The Ladybug

 The ladybug is sometimes called a <u>ladybird</u>. It is a very interesting insect. Most ladybugs are red or yellow with black spots. The California ladybug's shell is yellow with black spots. This beetle has a tiny head and no neck. Its body is round and shaped like half a pea. It can run very fast on its short legs. The ladybug's wings are tucked under its shell. It can fly very well.

The ladybug lays its eggs on the underside of green leaves. When the grubs hatch, they are very hungry. They quickly start to eat plant lice. Fruit growers like ladybugs because they eat harmful lice. Lice can ruin a farmer's crop.

The California ladybug was brought to the United States from Australia. It helps protect orange, lemon, and grapefruit trees.

1. What is <u>not</u> true about ladybugs?
   A. They have small heads.
   B. They have no neck.
   C. They can't fly.
   D. They can run fast.

2. Where does the ladybug lay its eggs?
   A. in a nest
   B. on the ground
   C. on the bark of a tree
   D. under a leaf

3. What do grubs eat?
   A. lice
   B. vegetables
   C. leaves
   D. fruit

4. What is another name for the ladybug?
   A. the love bug
   B. stinger
   C. spot
   D. ladybird

5. Match the word to its meaning.

   ___ grub   A. come from an egg

   ___ ladybug   B. a citrus fruit

   ___ lice   C. larva of a beetle

   ___ hatch   D. small insect pest

   ___ crops   E. farmer's plants

   ___ grapefruit   F. small beetle

Florida

Florida is located in the southeastern part of the United States. It is a <u>peninsula</u>. A peninsula is like an island because it is almost completely surrounded by water. But unlike an island, Florida is bordered by land on the northern part. Georgia and Alabama share borders with Florida. Spanish explorers settled in Florida. They called the area Florida because of all the flowers. <u>Florida</u> is a Spanish word for flowers.

This part of the United States is known for its warm climate and wonderful beaches. Florida's nickname is the Sunshine State. Because of the nice weather, it is a popular place to visit. Florida has grown over the years. Today, it is the home of several amusement parks.

Florida produces lots of food. It is best known for its fruit and fruit juices. Over half of the United States' orange and grape-fruit juice is processed in Florida. The warm climate allows the fruit to grow all year.

www.summerbridgeactivities.com

Reading Comprehension

1. Complete each sentence below.

<u>Florida</u> is a Spanish word for_____.

Florida is located in the_____ part of the

United States.

_____explorers were the first to settle in

Florida.

Florida produces a lot of_____.

2. What is a peninsula?

A. land that is almost completely surrounded by water

B. the Spanish word for "pencil"

C. the same thing as an island

3. Match the words in each column below to make
compound words.

south	fruit	_____
grape	shine	_____
sun	east	_____

4. Why does Florida produce so much fruit?

_____

_____

Ellis Island

Located in New York Harbor, Ellis Island was once used as an entrance to America. It was nicknamed the "Golden Door." Between 1897 and 1938, about 15 million people came from other countries to America. They came in search of religious freedom. They came in hopes of a <u>prosperous</u> new life. They came to find the "American Dream."

When people from other countries came to Ellis Island, they arrived by boat. These people were called immigrants. When the boats arrived at the island, immigration officers greeted the immigrants. Immigrants had to have health records and papers from their home countries. There were doctors giving physicals to verify the health records. Many immigrants passed the inspection and entered the United States, but others were sent away.

Many immigrants who entered the country were often disappointed. They didn't earn a lot of money and often had trouble finding places to live. They found that many Americans did not welcome them. They felt that they were not given the same rights as other Americans. It took many years for the immigrants to receive rights and <u>privileges</u> in the United States. Still, many immigrants felt the wait was worth it. Ellis Island is now a historical landmark.

1. What was Ellis Island?
   A. an island where immigrants live
   B. a door with golden arches
   C. the entrance to America for immigrants

2. What is an immigrant?
   A. an American citizen
   B. someone who comes from another country to America
   C. people who worked at Ellis Island

3. What does <u>prosperous</u> mean?
   A. rich in money, friends, and family
   B. safe
   C. good at your job

4. What does <u>privileges</u> mean?
   A. rights and opportunities
   B. misfortune
   C. rules to follow

5. Why do people from other countries come to America to live?

   _____

   _____

   _____

   _____

   _____

Chinese Immigrants

China is a very large country. There are many people living in China. In the late 1800s, overcrowded towns and villages in China meant there wasn't much food. The Chinese people were paying most of the money they earned to the government. They couldn't earn enough money to care for their families. During this time, many Chinese men moved to America with dreams of wealth and prosperity.

The Chinese men discovered that America wasn't the "Golden Door" they expected. Many Americans in the West were digging for gold. Many were striking it rich. The immigrants from China wanted to strike it rich, too. But the Chinese men weren't allowed to claim the gold. Some Americans would hire the Chinese men to dig for gold. They paid the Chinese men a very small salary, but they wouldn't let the Chinese immigrants have any rights to the gold. Many Chinese decided to start their own businesses. One type of business they were allowed to start was a laundry service.

The women remained in China to take care of the children and the family-owned land. As the children grew older, the boys were sent to the United States to work with their fathers and grandfathers.

1. What is the main idea of this story?

   A. Chinese immigrants in the 1800s found life in America difficult.

   B. China is a large country.

   C. Chinese men came to America without their wives.

   D. Many people were getting rich by digging for gold.

2. What does the word <u>profitable</u> mean?

   A. ability to make money

   B. ability to lose money

   C. ability to have money

3. What does the idiom "striking it rich" mean?

   A. becoming rich quickly

   B. losing a lot of money

   C. giving away a lot of money

4. Why were the Chinese men coming to America in the 1800s?

   _____

   _____

   _____

   _____

   _____

   _____

June 15, 1926

I am so excited. I am going to go with my grandfather to the New World. I had to beg my mother to allow me to go. I want to see my father. He has been in the New World for two years. I wonder what the New World is like. I wonder why my father left us to go to the New World.

June 20, 1926

This morning I said good-bye to my mother and grandmother. I said good-bye to my homeland, China. I will miss my mother and grandmother. I will miss China. My mother cried, and my grandmother went back inside the house. My grandfather and I got on a huge boat. It was the biggest boat I have ever seen. Many other people got on the boat, too. They are all going to the New World. Grandfather says that the trip will be long. Grandfather says I should be patient. I am not patient. I want to be in the New World now. I want to see my father. I want to help my father with his new laundry business.

August 5, 1926

We have finally reached America. The boat trip was harder than I expected. I became very sick, and I had to lie down most of the time. I miss my grandmother and mother. There are many people here. Everyone looks very different from people in my country. A doctor looked down my throat. Other people checked my paperwork and made my grandfather sign many papers. My grandfather told me to be polite. I tried to be polite, but it was hard. I want to see my father.

August 8, 1926

Today I found my father. He was glad to see us. We hugged and we cried. It was good to be in his arms again. He took us to his home. It had two bedrooms. Grandfather got his own bedroom, and Father and I share a room. I don't have any more time to write. Father is taking us to his shop to work. It is good to be in the New World. It is good to be with my father. I hope that my mother and grandmother will be coming to America soon.

Reading Comprehension

1. Why is Ling-Shau Yu writing a journal?

    A. He wants to tell about his trip to America.

    B. His mother wanted him to.

    C. He needs to practice his writing.

2. What is the New World?

    A. an undiscovered land

    B. China

    C. America

3. Complete each sentence below.

Ling-Shau's homeland is _____.

Ling-Shau's father started a _____business.

Ling-Shau traveled by_____to the New World.

Ling-Shau traveled with his_____to the New World.

4. Match the words in the two columns to make compound words. Write the words in the third column.

grand	room	_____
paper	mother	_____
bed	father	_____
grand	work	_____

5. In what year was this journal written?_____ What do you think happened in July of 1926 for Ling-Shau Yu?

_____

Riddle Reasoning

Read the riddles below. Draw your answers below each riddle.

What has eyes but cannot see?

What has horns but doesn't beep?

What kind of bird has wings but cannot fly?
(There are at least four answers.)

What kind of bed should you not sleep in?

What has a face but doesn't smile?

Rebus Fun

See if you can figure out what the "picture sentences" below are trying to say. Once you have figured out each one, write the words to form the sentences.

I love 2 swim. _____

Who R U? _____

I like 2 sing. _____

Do U like foot + ball? _____

Make your own "picture sentence" for the words below.

rainbow   sunglasses   friendship

Can you think of one on your own?

Make a Word

How many new words can you make using the letters in the words below? The first one is started for you.

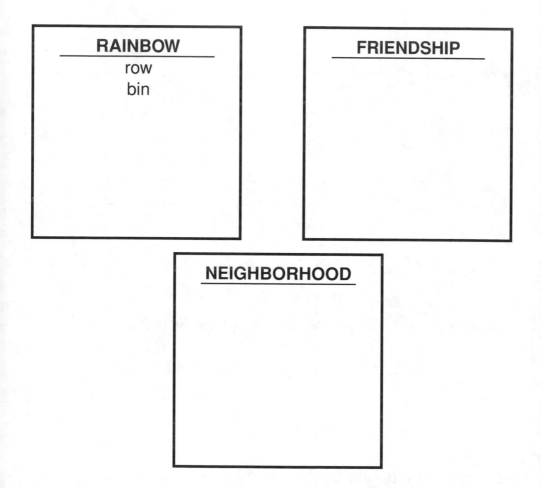

RAINBOW
row
bin

FRIENDSHIP

NEIGHBORHOOD

Make it a contest! Have a friend write the same three words down on a separate piece of paper and see who can come up with the most new words. Think of new words, and time yourselves to see who can get the most words the fastest!

Homonym Word Search

Write down a homonym for the words listed below. Then find and circle your answer in the word puzzle.

ate_____   bear_____

pear_____   blew_____

board_____   toe_____

sun _____   weak _____

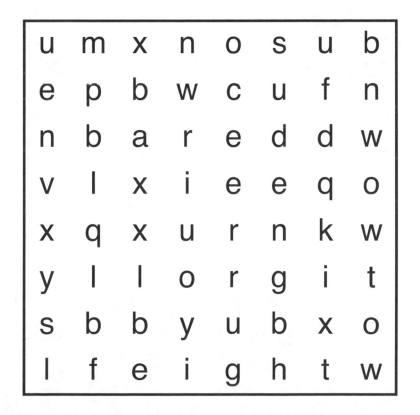

u	m	x	n	o	s	u	b
e	p	b	w	c	u	f	n
n	b	a	r	e	d	d	w
v	l	x	i	e	e	q	o
x	q	x	u	r	n	k	w
y	l	l	o	r	g	i	t
s	b	b	y	u	b	x	o
l	f	e	i	g	h	t	w

Koala Maze

What does a koala eat? Find your way through the maze to find out. Here are the rules: You can only cross over words that have more than one meaning. You can only cross over a word once. Good luck!

START HERE

star   sew   red

squash

raise

pear

bear

present   sky

Eucalyptus Leaves

fly   sail   board

ate

Pizza

seam

70

© RBP Books

Truck Repair

Look at the word inside each of the trucks. If the word inside the truck is the same spelled forwards and backwards, then you know that the truck works. If the word is different when it is spelled backwards, then you know that the truck doesn't work.

How many of the trucks below work?_____

How many don't work? _____

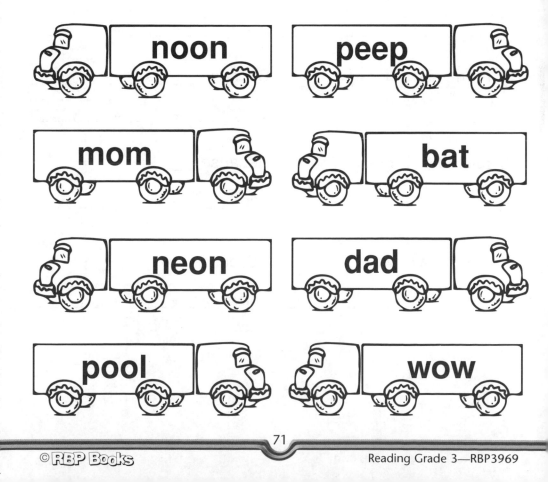

Reading Grade 3—RBP3969

Build a Word

The following words are out of order. Please put them in order so that they each make a compound word with the one before and after it.

Words:

   light   day   birth

Answer: **birth day light**   Because <u>birth</u> + <u>day</u> = <u>birthday</u>

and   <u>day</u> + <u>light</u> = <u>daylight</u>

Here are the rest:

1. suit   bathing   case   Because ____ + ____ = _____

_____ and ____ + ____ = _____

2. room   bed   flower   Because ____ + ____ = _____

_____ and ____ + ____ = _____

3. rain   tie   bow   Because ____ + ____ = _____

_____ and ____ + ____ = _____

4. door   way   ward   Because ____ + ____ = _____

_____ and ____ + ____ = _____

Fill in the Blanks

Fill in the blanks to make the words below complete. You must use the same two letters for the front and end of the words to make two complete words.

Example: __i__
nip
&
pin

Here are the words:

d ea **r**   __o__   __i__   __oo__   __a__   __a__   __o__

&   &   &   &   &   &   &

r ea **d**   __o__   __i__   __oo__   __a__   __a__   __o__

STAR spelled backwards makes RATS! Can you think of words that change when you spell them backwards to make new words? Write as many down here as you can.

_____

_____

_____

_____

_____

A Mixed Up Story

Read the sentences. Number them in the order in which they happened. Rewrite them in order on the lines below.

____ He put on his gloves and found a hoe.

____ She asked him to weed her flower garden.

____ Jim enjoyed weeding Mrs. Brown's beautiful garden.

____ He took his hoe and went home.

____ Jim wanted to weed the flower garden.

____ Mrs. Brown paid Jim $10.00.

____ He removed the weeds from his garden.

____ Mrs. Brown saw him weeding the flowers.

_____

_____

_____

_____

_____

_____

_____

_____

74

Answer Pages

Page 5
1. A
2. how to hit someone, how to call someone names, how to scream and shout when you are upset
3. laugh/cry, love/hate, work/rest, give/get, sad/happy
4. success

Page 7
1. A
2. calcium, vitamin C, folic acid, potassium, fiber
3. A
4. A
5. Answers will vary.

Page 9
1. A
2. C
3. C
4. Answers will vary.

Page 11
1. C   2. 3, 5, 1, 4, 2
3. D   4. Dad   5. F, F, T, F

Page 13
1. B   2. D   3. A
4. C   5. B

Page 15
1. C   2. C   3. A
4. find   5. Answers will vary.

Page 17
1. B   2. A   3. D
4. B

Page 19
1. C
2. circled words: without, handlebars, shoelaces, whenever
3. brakes, sense, pedals, road
4. Answers will vary.

Page 21
1. B
2. Answers will vary.
3. A
4. B
5. Answers will vary.

Page 23
1. B
2. B
3. pies, cherries, families, contests, washes, dishes
4. Answers will vary.

Page 25
1. a straight stick
2. straight up and down
3. B
4. A
5. Answers will vary.

Page 27
1. B
2. 5, 1, 2, 4, 3
3. B
4. A
5. hit the road/get going, talked my ear off/talked too much, shoot the breeze/talk about nothing in particular, time flies/time passes quickly

© RBP Books   Reading Grade 3—RBP3969

Answer Pages

Page 29
1. Answers will vary.
2. Answers will vary.
3. A
4. B
5. k, k, k, e, e, e

Page 31
1. He wrote books and newspaper articles. He helped write the Declaration of Independence. He made important discoveries about electricity.
2. He helped write the Declaration of Independence.
3. 5, 4, 2, 1, 3
4. Answers will vary.

Page 33
1. C   2. A   3. A
4. Answers will vary.
   Bonus! 13, 50

Page 35
1. B
2. graduate, celebrate, demonstrate, segregate
3. "I Have a Dream"
4. A
5. Answers will vary.

Page 37
1. A
2. land/sea, ground/sky, wild/tame, few/many, small/tall
3. name, game, small, tall, few, zoo, walk, flock, seas, trees, tame, name
4. A
5. Answers will vary.

Page 39
1. A
2. B
3. D
4. A

Page 41
1. A
2. tree house, headquarters, notebooks, clipboards, laptop, anywhere, everywhere, newspaper, backyard, first aid, heart attack
3. synonym, antonym, synonym, antonym, antonym, synonym
4. Answers will vary.

Page 43
1. D   2. B   3. A
4. ocean   5. C

Page 45
1. B
2. F, T, F, T
3. elephants/in groups, otters/floating on their backs, bats/upside down, flamingos/standing on one foot, squirrels/in nests in trees
4. Answers will vary.

Page 47
1. A
2. feathers; beaks, teeth; protective
3. A
4. B
5. Answers will vary.

Page 49
1. B
2. B
3. Answers will vary.
4. Answers will vary.

Answer Pages

Page 51
1. A
2. B, A, C, D, F, E
3. elf, pirate, fairy, place
4. Answers will vary.

Page 53
1. make-believe
2. A
3. C
4. Answers will vary.
5. Answers will vary.

Page 55
1. a creeper or a super-fast, super-sleek, big, squeaky chugger
2. C
3. A
4. Answers will vary.

Page 57
1. C
2. D
3. A
4. D
5. C, F, D, A, E, B

Page 59
1. flowers, southeastern, Spanish, food
2. A
3. southeast, grapefruit, sunshine
4. Answers will vary.

Page 61
1. C   2. B   3. A
4. A   5. Answers will vary.

Page 63
1. A   2. A   3. A
4. Answers will vary.

Page 65
1. A
2. C
3. China, laundry, boat, grandfather
4. grandmother, paperwork, bedroom, grandfather
5. 1926; answers will vary.

Page 66
a potato
a ram, goat, deer, etc.
penguin, ostrich, kiwi, emu
a flower bed
a clock

Page 67
I love to swim.
Who are you?
I like to sing.
Do you like football?
Answers will vary.

Page 68
Answers will vary.

Page 69
eight, bare, pair, blue, bored, tow, son, week

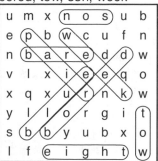

© RBP Books   Reading Grade 3—RBP3969

Answer Pages

Page 70

Page 71
Five of the trucks work:
    noon, peep, mom, dad, wow.
Three of the trucks do not work:
    bat, neon, pool.

Page 72
1. bathing suit case
2. flower bed room
3. rain bow tie
4. door way ward

Page 73
Answers will vary.
Some possibilities are:
    top & pot, pit & tip,
    loop & pool, tap & pat, bat & tab,
    now & won

Page 74
2, 5, 6, 8, 1, 7, 3, 4

Notes

Five things I'm thankful for:

1. _____
2. _____
3. _____
4. _____
5. _____

Notes

Five things I'm thankful for:

1. _____
2. _____
3. _____
4. _____
5. _____